Walt Whitman, Oscar Lovell Triggs

Selections from the Prose and Poetry of Walt Whitman

Walt Whitman, Oscar Lovell Triggs

Selections from the Prose and Poetry of Walt Whitman

ISBN/EAN: 9783744664721

Printed in Europe, USA, Canada, Australia, Japan

Cover: Foto ©Thomas Meinert / pixelio.de

More available books at **www.hansebooks.com**

SELECTIONS FROM
THE PROSE AND POETRY OF
WALT WHITMAN

Edited with an Introduction by
OSCAR LOVELL TRIGGS, PH.D.
(*The University of Chicago*)

SCIRE·QVOD
SCIENDVM

Boston
SMALL, MAYNARD & COMPANY
1898

GEO. H. ELLIS, PRINTER, 141 FRANKLIN STREET, BOSTON

PREFACE

The aim of the editor of this volume has been to make a representative selection from the prose and poetical writings of Walt Whitman. *He has tried to select, not what from a conventional point of view would be called " the best " of Whitman, but rather what is most characteristic in his writings.*

Among the prose compositions will be found the preface to the first edition of Leaves of Grass, *a remarkable essay, which, in its original form, has hitherto been inaccessible to the great majority of Whitman readers, and which is now printed verbatim et literatim from the text of the 1855 edition. In the choice of poems the effort has been made to preserve, in the character and arrangement of the pieces, the unitary conceptions which determined the architectonics of the last edition of* Leaves of Grass. *One or two letters have been added from the series written to Peter Doyle and to Whitman's mother during war-time. The biographical chapter was made up from many sources; but it relies for its authority chiefly upon the writings of Whitman's biographer and great friend, Dr. Richard Maurice Bucke. A series of notes and critical studies, at first announced for this volume, has been reserved for subsequent use; but a selected bibliography has been included for the convenience of students.*

O. L. T.

The University of Chicago,
March, 1898.

CONTENTS

WALT WHITMAN

I

Walt or Walter Whitman* (1819–1892) was born May 31, 1819, in West Hills, near Huntington, Long Island. While Walter was yet a child, the parents moved from West Hills to Brooklyn. The boy was educated at the Brooklyn Public Schools, tended in a lawyer's and a doctor's office, and was apprenticed at the printer's trade on *The Brooklyn Star* and *The Long Island Patriot*. He began at this time to write "sentimental bits" for the papers. At the age of sixteen he taught school in Long Island, "boarding round the district." For a year he published *The Long Islander* newspaper at Huntington. In 1840 he settled in New York City as printer and journalist, writing some essays and tales for *The Democratic Review*. In 1846 he became the editor of the daily paper, *The Brooklyn Eagle*. In 1848 he journeyed to New Orleans, and became a member of the editorial staff of *The Crescent*. In 1850 he was again in Brooklyn as the editor of *The Freeman*. From 1851 to 1854 he was engaged in the building trade in Brooklyn. During this period he was also writing, lecturing, and giving political talks. The first edition of *Leaves of Grass* appeared in 1855. The same year his father died. The second edition of the poems came out in 1856, and the third in 1860. In 1862 he went to the field of war, and engaged as a volunteer nurse in the hospital service. At the close of the war in 1865 he became a clerk in the office of the Secretary of the Interior, from which he was soon dismissed on the ground of being the author of "an indecent book," but was at once given a place in the office of the Attorney-General, which he kept till his illness in 1873. In 1865 (1866) he published *Drum-Taps* and other poems, including the Lincoln Hymn. The fourth edition of *Leaves of Grass* appeared in 1867. In 1871 he published *Democratic Vistas* and *Passage to India*. This year he wrote *After All not to Create Only*, and delivered it at the American Institute, New York. The fifth edition of *Leaves of Grass* was also issued in 1871. In 1872 he delivered *As a Strong Bird on Pinions Free* at the Commencement of Dartmouth

---

* He was called Walt to distinguish him from his father, Walter. Walter was signed to his first publications (see *The Death of Wind-foot, The American Review*, June, 1845), and in this name the copyright of *Leaves of Grass* in 1855 was taken out. In all later editions the name appears as Walt.

College, and travelled in the New England States. In 1873 he was prostrated by paralysis, and moved to Camden, New Jersey, where he resided, with spells of illness and recovery, until his death. The same year he suffered his greatest loss in the death of his mother. In 1874 he delivered *The Song of the Universal* at the Commencement of Tufts College. In 1875 *Memoranda of the War* was published. The sixth edition of *Leaves of Grass* and *Two Rivulets* (a supplementary volume) came out in 1876, the centennial year. In 1879 he travelled through the West and South, and the next year up through Canada. The seventh edition of the poems was issued in 1881; but the publication was abandoned by the publisher, James R. Osgood, of Boston, under threat of prosecution for issuing immoral literature. The eighth edition with final corrections was immediately set forth in Philadelphia in 1882, and in a separate volume the prose works entitled *Specimen Days and Collect*. *November Boughs*, poems and prose, appeared in 1888. The ninth edition of the *Leaves* and the complete prose writings were published in one volume in 1888–89. In 1889 a special autograph edition of the poems was made up. *Good Bye my Fancy* came out in 1891. The tenth edition of *Leaves of Grass* and the volume of prose were published in 1892. That year, 1892, on March 26, the poet died at Camden, and was buried in Harleigh Cemetery.

II

With reference to Whitman's life-work, the writing of *Leaves of Grass*, his career readily falls into four periods, each of which was distinguished by special experiences. The first and preparatory period extended from 1819 to 1855. The second or creative period included the years from 1855 to 1862, during which three editions of the poems appeared in rapid succession. The third extends from 1862 to 1873, which includes the experiences of the war and of his life at Washington, at which time his character culminated in its development of a universal sympathy. In 1873 he fell permanently ill. His writings passed continually under revision till the completion of the final edition the year of his death, in 1892.

III

The record of outer events does not constitute the biography of such a man as Whitman. He was a seer. His life was wrought in harmony with the higher spiritual laws of his being. What he contributed to the world was not a series of incidents, but a new spiritual experience.   By virtue of that experience his greatness is recognized and his power acknowledged.   He is to-day the minister of a religion whose service is admitted by palpable live disciples. Not to perceive the *sacer vates* aspect of his life is to miss the reason for his extraordinary influence and to remain ignorant of the essential fact of his biography.

IV

Leaves of Grass is Whitman's personal record.   It is a subtle and profound autobiography.   He himself composes the epic of the senses, the passions, the ideas, the spiritual aspirations the book displays.   Whether speaking of men, animals, or things, he has reference to himself, through whom the whole creation moves as in an endless procession.   The universe that he describes is the one he has personalized in his own consciousness.   This quality of the book is emphasized by the presence in every edition of something marked, as it were, "personal,"—an autograph, a portrait, a special note or poem.   The portrait facing the *Song of Myself* is, as Whitman said to his publisher, involved as part of the poem, an inherent part of his message to the world.

This characterization needs, however, some modification.   The poem is not in a narrow sense autobiographic.   While its first impression is that of a personality, the succeeding and dominant feeling is that of impersonality.   His " I " has an infinite range of meaning.   He stands as the type, the microcosmos, a man embracing all experiences natural to men and women.   His joys and sorrows, virtues and vices, are as often vicarious as personal.   " If you become degraded, criminal, ill, then I become so for your sake."   His experience furnishes a most remarkable proof of the possibility of identifying the individual with the universal man, and raises the question whether the true self is not in very fact the Spirit of the Universe.   His own soul in its growth took on impersonality.   He learned to speak of himself in an objective manner, the words " Walt Whitman " standing to him as a sign of the universal man.   " What am I," he once said, " but an idea, spirit — a new language for civilization ? "   In the last editions of his poems, passages referring to himself—as the lines in the *Song of the Broad-axe* descriptive of his own shape — were omitted.   During later years the perception grew that his work was especially representative.   In the note at the end of the 1889 edition of the Complete Works he queries: " The fancy rises whether the 33 years of life from 1855 to 1888, with their aggregate of our New World doings and people, created and formulated the works — coming actually from the direct urge and developments of those years, and not from any individual epic or lyrical attempts whatever, or from my pen or voice, or anybody's special voice, therefore considered as an autochthonic record and experience of the soul and evolution of America and of the world." It is better perhaps to conceive of Whitman not so much as a separate person as the representative of a cosmic instinct and tendency.

V

Nevertheless, the incarnated form and soul have to be considered, with their particular growths and experiences from the time of birth to death.

Walter was the second of a family of nine children,— seven boys and two girls. The Whitmans are English stock, the line in New England being directly traceable to the Rev. Zechariah Whitman (born 1595), who came from England in 1635, and settled at Milford, Connecticut. The Whitmans were men of considerable prominence in the colonial days. The Rev. Zechariah Whitman of Hull, Massachusetts, the nephew of the Milford Whitman, was a Harvard graduate (1668), and is described in the Dorchester records as " *Vir pius, humilis, orthodoxus, utilisimus.*" Joseph Whitman, of the Milford family, moved to Huntington, Long Island, about 1660, purchasing the farm at West Hills, which was occupied in turn by Whitman's great-grandfather, grandfather, and father. The family burying-ground, on the home farm, contains perhaps fifty stones, uninscribed as was the Quaker custom. The Whitman line is described as a long-lived race, large of stature, slow of movement, sturdy and friendly of nature. They appear to have been of democratic and heretical tendencies. In the Revolution several of the family were soldiers and officers of rank under Washington. Many members of the family have maintained the New England academic traditions, twelve of the name having graduated from Harvard, five at Yale, and nine at other Eastern colleges. There have been ministers and teachers beyond number. The great-grandmother on the paternal side is known to have been a large, swarthy woman, rather rude in disposition. The immediate grandmother, Hannah Brush, was a woman of superior type. With memories of the Revolution, she instilled into her grandson the spirit of independence. Walter Whitman, the poet's father (born 1789, died 1855), was a farmer and carpenter. He is pictured as a large, quiet, serious man, very kind to children and animals, good-natured, a good citizen, neighbor, and parent. His carpentry was solid and conscientious. His religious affinities were with the Quakers. The strong points of his character were resolution, love of freedom and independence.

The Van Velsors, the mother's family, were farmers and sailors of Holland-Dutch descent, having a homestead on Long Island at Cold Spring Harbor, some three miles distant from West Hills. The Van Velsors were generally warm-hearted, sympathetic, spiritual people. Major Cornelius was a jovial, free-hearted Americanized Netherlander, with his family passion for fine horses. The maternal grandmother was a woman of exceptional spiritual character. She was a member of the Society of Friends, and was deeply intuitive and of a kindly charitable disposition. Whitman draws her portrait in his poem on *Faces*: —

Behold a woman !
She looks out from her quaker cap, her face is clearer and more
    beautiful than the sky.
She sits in an armchair under the shaded porch of the farmhouse,
The sun just shines on her old white head.
Her ample gown is of cream-hued linen,
Her grandsons raised the flax, and her grand-daughters spun
    it with the distaff and the wheel.
The melodious character of the earth,
The finish beyond which philosophy cannot go and does not
    wish to go,
The justified mother of men.

Her name, Naomi Williams, suggests a Welsh or Celtic ancestry. The poet's mother, Louise, daughter of Cornelius Van Velsor, exhibits the best traits of the Holland woman, whose sign is a noble and perfect maternity. She was distinguished by sweetness of temper, sympathy, a genial optimism, and genuine spirituality of character. She was a hard worker, enjoyed splendid health, living to the age of eighty. Between her and Walt existed a strong and exceptional attachment. The poet always spoke of her as "dear, dear mother"; and of her and his sister Martha he said at the time of their death, in 1873, "They were the two best and sweetest women I have ever seen or known, or ever expect to see." It was undoubtedly from the mother that Whitman derived his essential nature. His due to her is acknowledged in his poem, *As at thy Portals also Death*: —

As at thy portals also death,
Entering thy sovereign, dim, illimitable grounds,
To memories of my mother, to the divine blending, maternity,
To her, buried and gone, yet buried not, gone not from me,
(I see again the calm benignant face fresh and beautiful still,
I sit by the form in the coffin,
I kiss and kiss convulsively again the sweet old lips, the cheeks,
    the closed eyes in the coffin;)
To her, the ideal woman, practical, spiritual, of all of earth,
    life, love, to me the best,
I grave a monumental line, before I go, amid these songs,
And set a tombstone here.

"As to loving and disinterested parents," Whitman has said, "no boy or man ever had more cause to bless and thank them than I." Of this inheritance of blood the Dutch ancestry is the most noticeable in Whitman's composition. He represents the Dutch-American type. He had the splendid health of the Netherlanders, their blond face, tinged with rose, gentle eyes, and flaxen hair, which turned to white at thirty. As evidences of Dutch origin, William Sloane Kennedy points to Whitman's endurance, practicality, sanity, thrift, excessive neatness and purity of person, and the preponderance of the simple and serious over the humorous and refined in his phrenology. The forms of his art are Dutch,— its realism, its glorification of the commonplace, its transcendentalism and mysticism. His independence is Dutch. In the vistas of his democratic ideas is discernible the struggle of the Netherlands for liberty, free thought, and free institutions. There is evidence of the mingling somewhere of French Protestant blood with the Dutch stock,— a common occurrence in early New York. The French terms in his writings appear to be home words rather than learned from books.

The Quaker traditions were strongly imposed upon his character. He had Quaker habits, such as wearing the hat and dressing in plain gray clothes. He had a dislike of ostentation or sensationalism. He wrote to Osgood, his publisher, to make his book "plain and simple even to Quakerism — no sensationalism about it — no luxury — a book for honest wear and use." Quaker traits appear in his silence, plainness, placidity, sincerity, self-respect, dislike of debate, strife, and war. They are evidenced in his friendliness, benevolence, his deep religiousness, and in his trust in the "Inner Light." The spirit both of the grandmother and mother descended upon him, directing his mind from childhood into spiritual channels. In the family and in the Long Island neighborhood the influence of Elias Hicks was strong and pervasive. The biography of Hicks that Whitman wrote in later life — loving and reverencing the great Quaker — is, as to spiritual matters, a transcript of the poet's own experiences. No one ever put greater trust in the authority of his own soul and interior revelation than he who defined the doctrine of the Quakers in these terms : " The great matter is to reveal and outpour the God-like suggestions pressing for birth in the soul." In the least thing or in the greatest Whitman waited for the promptings of the spirit, what he termed his " calls " or " summons." As a Quaker, he could not take part in internecine strife; but he felt " called " to go to the field to do what he could for the suffering sick and wounded of whatever army. To his friends assembled in 1889 to do him honor he said : " Following the impulse of the spirit (for I am at least half of Quaker stock) I have obeyed the command to come and look at you for a minute and show myself face to face ; which is probably the best I can do. But I have felt no command to make a speech ; and shall not therefore attempt any."

VI

Up to the age of twenty Whitman's environment was largely constituted by Long Island. Though his parents resided during most of this period at Brooklyn, yet the boy paid frequent visits to his relations at West Hills, taught school at sixteen in different parts of the island, " boarding round," and for a year or two edited at Huntington a newspaper, whose copies he distributed himself, walking or riding over the island.

Long Island was settled chiefly by the Dutch and English early in the seventeenth century. Their descendants, with some native Indians and a few negro slaves, constituted the population in Whitman's boyhood. Farming, ship-building, and fishing were the leading occupations. The island is about 120 miles long and 12 to 20 miles wide, in shape like a fish. Through the centre runs an irregular range of low hills, affording every variety of scenery. The coast line is indented with harbors. These and the salt marshes at the upper reaches of the inlets give characteristic touches to an island home. The hills are fully wooded with trees of oak, hickory, pine, chestnut, and locust. The farm-houses are generally low frame structures, covered roof and sides with shingles that have weathered to a soft gray. About the hamlets are abundant orchards. Lilacs grow in every dooryard. The island is noted for its streams, its diminutive lakes, and its springs of cold water. The hermit-thrush is vocal in its woods. The general features of the landscape are irregularity, undulation, vista. These appear to be the very forms in which Whitman's thought is cast.

At West Hills he had as concrete background the gently rolling country-side and views of the sea. The homestead was so named because of its situation in the midst of the group of hills which form the western portion of the island. Near the home rose Jaynes Hill, the highest point of land in Long Island, in height some 350 feet, from the summit of which is an extensive and picturesque prospect of the undulating hills and plains, the gleaming sound, and the white breakers of the sea. At the foot of the hill the Whitman homestead was situated. A view of the original home and the domestic interior is furnished by John Burroughs in one of his early notes : " The Whitmans lived in a long story-and-a-half farm-house, hugely timbered. A great smoke-canopied kitchen, with vast hearth and chimney, formed one end of the house. The existence of slavery in New York at that time, and the possession by the family of some twelve or fifteen slaves, house and field servants, gave things quite a patriarchal look. The very young darkies could be seen, a swarm of them, toward sundown, in the kitchen, squatted in a circle on the floor, eating their supper of Indian pudding and milk. In the house, and in food and furniture, all was rude, but substantial. No carpets nor stoves were known, and no coffee, and tea and sugar only for the women. Rousing wood fires gave both warmth and light on winter nights. Pork, poultry, beef, and all the ordinary vegetables and grains were plentiful. Cider was the men's common drink, and used at meals. The clothes were mainly homespun. Journeys were made by both men and women on horseback. Books were scarce. The annual copy of the Almanac was a treat, and was pored over through the long winter evenings.'' Parts of this primitive cabin are still standing. Near by is a large oak-tree and a grove of black walnuts. Beyond the house a stream flows down from the hills eastward across the plains. About a mile to the east Whitman's parents resided. Of this scene at West Hills, Daniel G. Brinton has recorded his impression : " Here on this spot, I believe I caught what I had hoped I might — the inspiration of the scene, which, unconsciously to himself, had moulded Walt's mind. I say unconsciously, for once I asked him whether the landscapes of his boyhood still haunted his dreams and formed the settings and frames of his nightly visions, as mine do with me ; but he returned one of those steady glances and vague replies with which he was wont to turn aside the curious, leaving me in doubt whether such was not the case, or whether I had approached with shodden feet some holy ground in the fane of his mind.   Whatever the answer might have been, now I know that·the peasant sturdiness of that landscape, its downright lines, its large sweeps, its lack of set forms, created the mould into which his later thought was cast. Neither years of wider life nor witnessing grander beauties altered him from what the West Hills had made him.''

Cold Spring village, the home of the Van Velsors, is wilder and more romantic in its view of sea and shore.   It is noted for its shipping and its sailors.   This locality and the maternal homestead may be described in Whitman's own words, written while on a visit to the scene of his youth : —

'' I write this paragraph on the burial hill of the Van Velsors near Cold Spring, the most significant depository of the dead that could be imagined, without the slightest help from art, soil sterile, a mostly bare plateau-flat of an acre, the top of a hill, brush and well-grown trees and dense woods bordering all around, very primitive, secluded, no visitors, no road (you cannot drive here, you have to bring the dead on foot, and follow on foot). Two or three-score graves quite plain ; as many more almost rubbed out.   My grandfather Cornelius and my grandmother Amy (Naomi) and numerous relatives nearer or remoter, on my mother's side, lie buried here.   The scene as I stood or sat, the delicate and wild odor of the woods, a slightly drizzling rain, the emotional atmosphere of the place, and the inferred reminiscences, were such as I never realized before.

'' I went down from this ancient grave-place eighty or ninety rods to the site of the Van Velsor homestead, where my mother was born (1795), and where every spot had been familiar to me as a child and youth (1825–'40).   Then stood there a long rambling dark-gray, shingle-sided house, with sheds, pens, a great barn and much open road-space.   Now of all these not a vestige left ; all had been pulled down, erased, and the plough and harrow passed over foundations, road-spaces and everything for many summers ; fenced in at present, and grain and clover growing like any other fine fields.   Only a big hole from an ancient cellar, with some little heaps of broken stone, green with grass and weeds, identified the place.   Even the great old brook and spring seemed to have mostly dwindled away.

"In some particulars this whole scene, with what it aroused, memories of my young days there half a century ago, the vast old kitchen and ample fireplace and the sitting-room adjoining, the plain furniture, the meals, the house full of merry people, my grandmother Amy's sweet old face in its Quaker cap, my grandfather 'the Major,' jovial, red, stout, with sonorous voice and characteristic physiognomy, made perhaps the most pronounced half-day's experience of my whole jaunt."

Of the general region Whitman has said : "How well I remember the region—the flat plains with their prairie like vistas and grassy patches in every direction, and the 'kill-calf,' and herds of cattle and sheep.   Then the South shores and the salt meadows and the sedgy smell, and numberless little bayous and hummock-islands in the waters, the habitat of every sort of fish and aquatic fowl of North America.   And the bay men — a strong, wild, peculiar race — now extinct, or rather wholly changed.   And the beach outside the sandy bars, with their old historic wrecks and storms — the weird white-gray beach — not without its tales of pathos — tales too of grandest heroes and heroisms."

In the midst of a sturdy agricultural community, and in association with farmers, pilots, and fishermen, Whitman spent thus much of his youth.   He enjoyed the freedom of life in the open air. Neighbors remember him as a free-hearted and rollicking boy, broad-shouldered, nonchalant, a leader among his fellows.   He dressed and looked like a "water dog."   One sea-captain said of the young Whitman at Huntington, "I can smell salt water ten miles away on just seeing him."   His boyhood memories were of swimming, boating, clam-digging, gathering sea-gulls' eggs, of light-house and pilot boat, of the farm life, and of the herdsmen and Indians of the interior.

With the associations of the homestead his poems are saturated. He acknowledges his origin in the poem beginning, "Starting from fish-shape Paumanok where I was born."   In *There was a Child Went Forth* the memories are all of his own boyhood, the associations either of Long Island or Brooklyn.   As he was gifted with large receptivity, the capacity to affiliate with men and objects in multitudes, the extent of his absorption of his early environment can never be fully measured.   His love of the sea, the salt and sedge of his works, and his sense of the mystic meaning of the wave pushing upon the shore, moaning, and casting up drift-wood, were gained at this time. The identification of himself with animals and all evolutionary growths was no doubt a life-long experience. To the sun he said, "Always I have loved thee, even as basking babe, then happy boy alone by some wood edge, thy touching-distant beams enough, or man matured or young or old." Other details of early perception are revealed in *There was a Child Went Forth:*—

The early lilacs became part of this child,
The grass and white and red morning-glories, and white and red clover, and the song of the phœbe-bird,
And the Third-month lambs and the sow's pink-faint litter, and the mare's foal and the cow's calf,
And the noisy brood of the barnyard or by the mire of the pond side,
And the fish suspending themselves so curiously below there, and the beautiful curious liquid,
And the water plants with their graceful flat heads, all became part of him.

The hurrying tumbling waves, quick-broken crests, slapping,
The strata of color'd clouds, the long bar of maroon-tint away solitary by itself, the spread of purity it lies motionless in,
The horizon's edge, the flying sea-crow, the fragrance of salt marsh and shore mud,
These became part of that child.

It was indeed on Long Island that much of his first work was written. He told a friend that he went down on Long Island on a cold, bleak promontory, where but one farmer resided, and lived there while *Leaves of Grass* was gestating. There he wrote his first copy, and threw it into the sea.

VII

Two great races of Northern Europe, it will be seen, combined to produce a typical man : the Dutch contributed the more per-sonal habits and traits, the English, sturdiness, force, and wilfulness. An inheritance of Quaker spirituality made complete the character on the religious and intuitive side. Heredity and training accrue thus far to democracy. Whitman was born of the people, of lib-eral and revolutionary stock. Political aristocracy had no part in his making. His ancestry and training are paralleled by that of

Lincoln and Grant, who sprang directly from the mass, and represent therefore the advance of humanity as a whole. If we were to prophesy from the beginning, it might be averred that Whitman, by birth and education, was singularly capacitated to become the poet of the Body and the Soul. His splendid health, life out of doors, power of sense absorption, would render him able to sing the "joys of mere living." Home ties, deep human sympathies, the democracy of the father, the intuition of the mother, the spirit of the simple Quaker homestead, the habit of communion with nature, would tend to make him the poet of the Soul.

VIII

A few early associations belong to Brooklyn. He attended the public schools of that city at intervals until he was about fourteen years of age, when he became apprenticed to the trade of printing in the office of *The Brooklyn Star*. One item of his childhood is worth mentioning, since the incident links the poet with our national life. On the visit of Lafayette to this country in 1825 he assisted at the dedication of a public library in Brooklyn. On that occasion, while helping some children to a convenient place for witnessing the ceremony, Lafayette took up the child Walter, then about five years old, held him in his arms, and kissed him. As a boy, too, he spent much time at the river docks among the shipping and listening to the tales of the seamen. Such association formed no inconsiderable part of his education ; for the seamen of that day, as John Swinton asserts, were men of tougher stock than those of the present,—brainy, thoroughly American, literally children of the Revolution.

The New York period, from about 1840 to 1862, is most significant with regard to Whitman's real education. The years from 1840 to 1855 were the decisive ones in the formation of his character and in the preparation for the task of writing *Leaves of Grass*. These fifteen years of miscellaneous occupation constituted his apprenticeship to poetry. Altogether it was an education that exceeded in its results the conscious training of any other poet of the century. He spent his life on the Open Road, absorbing the outside shows, reading inarticulate objects as others read the pages of books. Many a day was spent on the ferries, or in sailing out to sea with the pilots, or in riding upon the omnibuses through the streets "with their turbulent musical chorus." "I suppose the critics may laugh," Whitman once said, "but the influence of those Broadway omnibus jaunts and drives, and declamations, and escapades, undoubtedly entered into the gestation of *Leaves of Grass.''* It was his purpose to sound all the experiences of life. He experimented in unwonted ways. He visited hospitals, almshouses, prisons, and the haunts of vice. He attended churches, lectures, debates, political meetings, read at libraries, studied at museums, spoke sometimes in debate, having trained himself as an orator. He made himself familiar with all kinds of employments, became intimate with laborers, business men, merchants, and men of letters. He was a constant attender at the leading New York theatres and opera houses, hearing every important actor and singer of the time. He was especially affected by the elder Booth and by Alboni. His love of music, an elemental passion, was fully gratified in New York. *Proud Music of the Storm,* written in 1871, shows a perfect intimacy with the method and content of music : —

All senses, shows and objects, lead to thee, O soul,
But now it seems to me sound leads o'er all the rest.

'' Give me,'' he exclaims, '' to hold all sounds.''

Fill me with all the voices of the universe,
Endow me with their throbbings, Nature's also,
The tempests, waters, winds, operas and chants, marches and
    dances,
Utter, pour in, for I would take them all !

In New York he witnessed all the national movements of the day. He saw or heard Andrew Jackson, Webster, Clay, Seward, Van Buren, Kossuth, Halleck, the Prince of Wales, Dickens, and other celebrities. One of his reminiscences refers to John Jacob Astor The year 1853 was signal as being the World's Fair year in New York, and the Exposition opened infinite opportunities to the eager Whitman. Through these years his curiosity was unbounded. His interests were absolutely universal, and his absorptive power was limited only by the things to be observed. Withal he accomplished, in an almost secret way, much careful reading and study. He collected immense scrap-books of articles on all manner of subjects, made abstracts of books and lectures, wrote out outlines of original lectures on history, philosophy, and politics. He was everywhere observant, absorbent, reflective, thoughtful. His enormous knowledge, universal sympathies, and serene wisdom were gained during this poetic apprenticeship. Out of the vision

which the soul saw of life in the mirror of the world Whit-
man's poems were composed. For an occupation he engaged
in journalism, editing at different times *The Brooklyn Eagle* and
The Freeman. At other times he took up house-building, aban-
doning this occupation after a few years, when it had become too
exacting and remunerative. In 1849 he began his *Wanderjahren*,
travelling through the Central West and the South. He remained
in New Orleans a year on the staff of the *Crescent* newspaper. In
his journeys through the States he found "wonders, revelations,
the real America." In travel he gathered materials with boundless
curiosity. No one can know what multitudes went to the making
of the composite Democratic Individual that uttered *The Song of
Myself*.

While editor of *The Freeman*, he became one of the leading
members of the group of New York Bohemians that met nightly
at Pfaff's restaurant on Broadway to celebrate nationality in litera-
ture and art. For the decade preceding the war, *The Saturday
Press*, assisted by the comic *Vanity Fair* under the editorship of
Charles Farrar Browne, or "Artemus Ward," embodied the new
literary movement of the city. With plenty of wit and cleverness,
and some cynicism, the writers of these journals led the attack
against literary shams. Among the Pfaffian group were Fitz-James
O'Brien, Fitzhugh Ludlow, Aldrich, Stedman, William Winter,
Ned Wilkins, George Arnold, Gardette, "Artemus Ward," Ada
Clare, the "Queen," and a score of others. The order had been
established by Henry Clapp, who transplanted from Paris the
moods and methods of Bohemia on the pattern of Henry Mürger's
Vie de Bohème. Of this group Whitman was a recognized leader.
Some of his stories were written at the hall of meeting. In one of
his note-books is a rough sketch of a poem, beginning, "The vault
at Pfaff's where the drinkers and laughers meet to eat and drink
and carouse," and closing : "You phantoms ! oft I pause, yearn to
arrest some one of you ! Oft I doubt your reality, suspect all is
but a pageant." In an interview published in *The Brooklyn Eagle*
in 1886, Whitman gives an account of the meetings : "I used to
go to Pfaff's nearly every night. It used to be a pleasant place to go
in the evening after finishing the work of the day. When it began
to grow dark, Pfaff would invite everybody who happened to be
sitting in the cave he had under the sidewalk to some other part of
the restaurant. There was a long table extending the length of
the cave ; and as the Bohemians put in an appearance Henry
Clapp would take a seat at the head of the table. I think there

was as good talk around that table as took place anywhere in the world. Clapp was a very witty man. Fitz-James O'Brien was very bright. Ned Wilkins, who used to be the dramatic critic of *The Herald*, was another bright man. There were between twenty-five or thirty journalists, authors, artists, and actors who made up the company that took possession of the cave under the sidewalk.''

During this period Whitman remained in perfect health. He seemed to be as finely related to Nature by his exquisite senses and physical constitution as he was to spiritual facts by his mentality. Constant communication with the sea, observation of the night and stars, affiliation with the woods and winds and the broad day, taught him the lore that gave lessons to daily living and to all else. When in 1873 he suffered paralysis and turned in his loneliness to record the doings of nature in and about Camden, it is impossible not to see that observation and absorption of nature were habitual with him from childhood.

In the midst of these years one incident of his real biography appears,— the only fact, perhaps, worthy of report,— the one that gives meaning to his life, explains his poems, and certifies to his right to immortality. About the year 1850, apparently as the result of a momentary inspiration, in reality as issue of a life perfected symmetrically in every faculty of being, physical and psychical, some inner change of consciousness, some increase in ideal experience, some accession of power, took place. The nature of the experience cannot be fully described, though the phenomenon is not new in the history of the world. One becomes aware of the attainment of a higher consciousness, of passage into a region where new motives form and new knowledge accrues. Mr. Stedman, somewhat lightly, though with his eye on the fact, gives testimony that Whitman ''underwent conversion, experienced a change of thought and style, and professed a new departure in verse, dress, and way of life.'' Dr. Richard Maurice Bucke, with a truer insight into the nature of the revelation, relying on the phenomenon of exceptional development which Whitman presents in respect to physical, intellectual, moral, and emotional stature, seeing clearly that such experience constitutes an evolutionary advance in the human world, a new variety or species of mental wisdom, advances the theory that Whitman, at this period, rose into a higher state of consciousness, which may be called ''cosmic,'' by which is meant that to the ordinary self-consciousness there was added a higher form, which includes the knowledge of life, death, immortality, and the cosmical order. Upon the fact of a new and superior reading of the universe, Whitman bases his enormous claims for recognition.

> I too, following many and follow'd by many, inaugurate a relig-
>   ion, I descend into the arena,
> (It may be I am destin'd to utter the loudest cries there, the
>   winner's pealing shouts,
> Who knows ? they may rise from me yet, and soar above every-
>   thing.)
>
> Each is not for its own sake,
> I say the whole earth and all the stars in the sky are for relig-
>   ion's sake.

If *Leaves of Grass* is not something more than a new collation of phrases, if it is not something more than a new literary method, if it does not embody a new human experience, if it is not a new interpretation of the facts of existence, if it is not a new revelation of truth, then it is without meaning, and doomed soon to pass utterly away. A mere trick of speech can have no permanent influence on the world. But the book appears to be the work of one who has suddenly advanced into a new circle of knowledge. From 1850 to 1855 Whitman was absorbed in the contemplation and investigation of the newly revealed world of his being. He gave up all other occupation, under the compulsion of a new ideal, and became a solitary, seeking in secret some recess in the woods or by the sea that he might jot down with more absolute precision the passing events of his experience. " You contain enough Walt," the new Genius kept saying, "why don't you let it out, then ? " It was true. The man had content for prophecy.

> I lie abstracted and hear beautiful tales of things and the reasons
>   of things,
> They are so beautiful I nudge myself to listen.
>
> I cannot say to any person what I hear — I cannot say it to
>   myself — it is very wonderful.

The consciousness to which he had now arrived may well be called " cosmic," for it is always to cosmic unity that his most mystic and prophetic poems refer.

> I sing to the last the equalities modern or old.

I sing the endless finalés of things,
I say Nature continues, glory continues,
I praise with electric voice,
For I do nat see one imperfection in the universe,
And I do not see one cause or result lamentable at last in the
universe.

Knowing the cosmical integrity, he can sing under the sun
unmitigated adoration : "All is truth without exception." "And
henceforth I will go celebrate anything I see or am, and sing and
laugh and deny nothing." One section of the *Song of Myself,*
the fifth, must refer to the new revealment : —

Swiftly arose and spread around me the peace and knowledge
that pass all the argument of the earth,
And I know that the hand of God is the promise of my own,
And I know that the spirit of God is the brother of my own,
And that all the men ever born are also my brothers, and the
women my sisters and lovers,
And that a kelson of the creation is love,
And limitless are leaves stiff or drooping in the fields,
And brown ants in the little wells beneath them,
And mossy scabs of the worm fence, heap'd stones, elder, mul-
lein and poke-weed.

Such utterance is not wholly new in literature. Immortality
has been held as a dogma for many centuries. Evil has been
pronounced null, and love declared to be universal. But Whit-
man differs from all others in the certainty of his knowledge. He
does not speculate about love and death. He knows he is an
immortal soul. His surety is grounded in consciousness. This
"conversion," at about the age of thirty, is the most important
fact in Whitman's biography. *Leaves of Grass* can be accounted
for on no other ground than that it was the product of what we
call "genius," or "inspiration."

IX

In 1862 Whitman, on hearing that his brother George had
been wounded at Fredericksburg, started for the army camp, then
on the Rappahannock. Finding his brother out of danger, he re-
mained on the field of war ; but, as he did not feel "called" to
carry arms, his mission not being to fight, but to save, he engaged
as a volunteer in the hospital service. In this occupation he re-

mained till the close of the war, and as long thereafter as his office was needed. During this period he supported himself as a war correspondent to Northern papers and by copying in offices, until, in 1865, he was tendered a clerkship in a government department. As an army nurse, he is reported as having made upward of six hundred visits or tours, tended a hundred thousand soldiers, and distributed many thousands of dollars, the gifts of Northern friends. It is difficult to describe the agency of the poet in the office of nurse. The numerical account of his cases gives no idea of the personal character of his ministration. The methods he employed for restoring health and healing were characteristic of the man. He performed the ordinary function of the physician and nurse, but beyond these by a few simple expedients he accomplished more remarkable results by quietly affecting the spiritual nature of the men. "To many of the wounded and sick, especially the youngsters," he said, "there is something in personal love, caresses and the magnetic flood of sympathy and friendship, that does, in its way, more good than all the medicines in the world. The American soldier is full of affection, and the yearning for affection. And it comes wonderfully grateful to him to have this yearning gratified when he is laid up with wounds or illness, far away from home, among strangers. Many will think this merely sentimentalism, but I know it is the most solid of facts. I believe that even the moving around among the men, or through the ward, of a hearty, healthy, clean, strong, generous-souled person, man or woman, full of humanity and love, sending out invisible, constant currents thereof, does immense good to the sick and wounded." So he came into their presence always buoyant and cheerful, and sought particularly to satisfy their affectionate longings. He was physician, nurse, and mother to all. The external details of his ministry are vividly reported in one of the poems of the *Drum-Taps* series : —

Bearing the bandages, water and sponge,
Straight and swift to my wounded I go,
Where they lie on the ground after the battle brought in,
Where their priceless blood reddens the grass the ground,
Or to the rows of the hospital tent, or under the roof'd hospitals,
To the long rows of cots up and down each side I return,
To each and all one after another I draw near, not one do I miss.

I onward go, I stop,
With hinged knees and steady hand to dress wounds,

I am firm with each, the pangs are sharp yet unavoidable,
One turns to me his appealing eyes — poor boy ! I never knew
you,
Yet I think I could not refuse this moment to die for you, if that
would save you.

But this is not the whole account. He was seen in 1863 by
Mr. Burroughs, who made at the time the following note: "The
actual scene of this man moving among the maimed, the pale, the
low-spirited, the near-to-death, with all the incidents and the
interchange between him and those suffering ones, often young
almost to childhood, can hardly be pictured by any pen, however
expert. His magnetism was incredible and exhaustless. It is no
figure of speech, a fact deeper than speech. The lustreless eye
brightened up at his approach; his commonplace words invigorated;
a bracing air seemed to fill the ward and neutralize the bad smells."
To the same effect is the report of an eye-witness who wrote in *The
New York Herald* in 1876 an account of what he saw in the hos-
pitals: "When Whitman appeared, in passing along, there was a
smile of affection and welcome on every face, however wan, and
his presence seemed to light up the place as it might be lit by the
presence of the Son of Love. From cot to cot they called him,
often in tremulous tones or in whispers ; they embraced him,
they touched his hand, they gazed at him. To one he gave a
few words of cheer, for another he wrote a letter home, to others
he gave an orange, a few comfits, a cigar, a pipe and tobacco,
a sheet of paper, or a postage stamp, all of which, and many other
things, were in his capacious haversack. From another he would
receive a dying message for mother, wife, or sweetheart; for
another he would promise to go on an errand; to another, some
special friend, very low, he would give a manly farewell kiss.
He did the things for them which no nurse or doctor could do,
and he seemed to leave a benediction at every cot as he passed
along. The lights had gleamed for hours in the hospital that
night before he left it; and, as he took his way toward the door,
you could hear the voice of many a stricken hero calling, 'Walt,
Walt, Walt, come again.'" One characteristic incident, illus-
trative of the silent sympathy existing between nurse and patient, is
told by Whitman himself of a youth who, as the poet sat looking
at him while he lay asleep, suddenly, without the least start,
awakened, opened his eyes, gave him a long steady look, turning
his face very slightly to gaze easier,— one long clear silent look,—

a slight sigh,— then turned back and went into his doze again.
"Little he knew," the poet added, "poor, death-stricken boy,
the heart of the stranger that hovered near." The mystic inter-
pretation of some such incident is given in O *Tan-Faced Prairie-
Boy* : —

> You came, taciturn, with nothing to give — we but look'd on
>   each other,
> When lo! more than all the gifts of the world you gave me.

The issues of the war to Whitman were many. His character
was rounded full circle by devotional service. His knowledge of
life was infinitely extended. He became the high priest of pain
and the apostle of love. The war brought to maturity his large
emotional nature, arousing, bringing out, and deciding undreamed
of depths of affection. To his dying day he remembered the
"experience sweet and sad" that

> Many a soldier's loving arms about this neck have cross'd and
>   rested,
> Many a soldier's kiss dwells on these bearded lips.

He wished his name might be published as that of the tenderest
lover. He sought friends who were not proud of his songs, but of
the measureless ocean of love within him.

> Beauty, knowledge, inure not to me — yet there are two or three
>   things inure to me,
> I have nourish'd the wounded and sooth'd many a dying soldier,
> And at intervals waiting or in the midst of camp,
> Composed these songs.

> Dearest comrades, all is over and long gone,
> But love is not over — and what love, O comrades !
> Perfume from battle-fields rising, up from the fœtor arising.

> Perfume therefore my chant, O love, immortal love,
> Give me to bathe the memories of all dead soldiers,
> Shroud them, embalm them, cover them all over with tender pride.

> Perfume all — make all wholesome,
> Make these ashes to nourish and blossom,
> O love, solve all, fructify all with the last chemistry.

> Give me exhaustless, make me a fountain,

That I exhale love from me wherever I go like a moist perennial
  dew,
For the ashes of all dead soldiers South or North.

The war was his tutor in democracy. His "most fervent
views of the true *ensemble* and extent of the States" were gained
at this event. He studied Lincoln closely, and caught the deep
though subtle and indirect expression of his face. He observed
the heroism of soldiers marching to the front, returning from battle,
dying on the field or in hospitals, displaying under all circumstances
the utmost faith and fortitude, in life courageous, in death sublime.
The people were tested, and personality put to proof. He became
proud of the armies,—"the noblest that ever marched."

Race of veterans — race of victors !
Race of the soil, ready for conflict — race of the conquering
  march !
(No more credulity's race, abiding-temper'd race,)
Race henceforth owning no law but the law of itself,
Race of passion and the storm.

The race was proven capable of making sacrifices for an ideal
purpose. He perceived the new chivalry arising, the chivalry of
comradeship. He saw that love lay latent in all hearts, and that
a practical comradeship already existed among men. "In the
hospitals," he wrote in 1863, "among the American soldiers,
East and West, North and South, I could not describe to you
what mutual attachments, passing deep and tender. Some have
died, but the love for them lives so long as I draw breath. The
soldiers know how to love too, when once they have the right
person. It is wonderful. You see I am running off into the
clouds (perhaps my element)."
The war again was the occasion of his own physical prostration,
the checking of his enormous vitality at its high tide. He said he
volunteered as a nurse because he was so strong and well. But in
1864 the strain, emotional as well as physical, began to tell on
him. In 1865 he suffered a temporary prostration, due to malaria
and to blood-poisoning absorbed from gangrenous wounds. A
slight paralytic attack occurred in 1870. In 1873 he was com-
pletely prostrated by paralysis, complicated by malaria and blood-
poisoning. He was brought to Camden, New Jersey, where he
lived in retirement till the end, with spells of illness and returning

strength, never for any time freed from physical debility and the inertia of paralysis. The history of the war contains no nobler instance of sacrifice.

The war tested his religion and faith. He was able to give a practical demonstration of his principles of democracy by realizing concretely with thousands of men the joy of manly attachment. The war tried his sanity, his cheerfulness, his faith and optimism, his own essential goodness and charity. In all trials his life was a practical commentary on the book he was writing.

Lastly, the war supplied him with themes for the sweetest and purest of his poems, and incidents and thoughts for the most representative of his prose writings. The *Drum-Taps* and the poems on Lincoln, unique in their imaginative and spiritual suggestiveness, which contain perhaps the most thrilling summons to arms and at the same time the most deeply moving aspects of suffering and death ever presented in song, were published in 1865, the immediate output of the conflict. *Democratic Vistas*, his most considerable prose work, appeared in 1871, embodying the thoughts tha sprang from the emotions stirred by the sight of "warlike America rising and breaking chains." His *Memoranda of the War*, first published in 1875, but written from day to day on the spot of encounter in a vivid, short-hand, impressionistic style, contains the most thrilling and powerful descriptions of battle and hospital scenes that the war records afford. Poems and memoranda, written on odd scraps of paper and in blood-smutched note-books, breathe the very atmosphere of the moment and incident. Collectively, these works completely identify the age of Lincoln, with its characteristic scenes, passions, ideas, and flame-like results. Finally, a new interpretation was given to life and the world, the "mystic army" and the "mighty bivouac-field and waiting-camp of all."

As I ponder'd in silence,
Returning upon my poems, considering, lingering long,
A Phantom arose before me with distrustful aspect,
Terrible in beauty, age, and power,
The genius of poets of old lands,
As to me directing like flame its eyes,
With finger pointing to many immortal songs,
And menacing voice, *What singest thou?* it said,
Know'st thou not there is but one theme for ever-enduring bards?
And that is the theme of War, the fortune of battles,
The making of perfect soldiers.

Be it so, then I answer'd,
*I too haughty Shade also sing war, and a longer and greater one
than any,
Waged in my book with varying fortune, with flight, advance
and retreat, victory deferr'd and wavering,
(Yet methinks certain, or as good as certain, at the last,) the
field the world,
For life and death, for the Body and for the eternal Soul,
Lo, I too am come, chanting the chant of battles,
I above all promote brave soldiers.*

And then —

Presently O soldiers, we too camp in our place in the bivouac-
camps of green,
But we need not provide for outposts, nor word for the counter-
sign,
Nor drummer to beat the morning drum.

X

Summarizing at this point Whitman's historical relations, it may
be said that he connects the two great eras of American history,—
the era of independence centering in the Revolutionary War and
the era of social union that concentrated in the Civil War; and he
connects them with a completeness and integrity that can be pre-
sumed of no other American author. And he not only connects
the eras historically, but he embodies their results in his own per-
sonality. As a child, he received the traditions of the Revolution
from those who had participated in the struggle. These traditions
related to independence, self-assertion, and pride. They constitute
the first principle of a democratic philosophy and the first factor of
its practical polity. Whitman himself was a sharer in the toils of
the war for union. He became its chief singer, and was the lead-
ing spokesman of reconciliation. The second great principle of
democracy is love, whose concrete form is federation and union.
Leaves of Grass, having as its key-words pride and love, is the
exact counterpart of American history thus far. Whitman is the
genius of American nationality.

XI

In 1873, on the occasion of his illness, Whitman removed to
Camden, where he continued to reside until his death. With this
period no important outward event is associated. The poet, often

solitary, harassed by pain, grew and ripened inwardly, associating with nature, men, and books. "I came to Camden to die," he said, "but every day I went into the country and naked bathed in sunshine, lived with the birds and squirrels, and played in the water with the fishes. I recovered my health from Nature — strange how she carries us through periods of infirmity out into the realms of freedom and health." One of his favorite resorts was Timber Creek, near the Delaware, a place that provided him with "primitive solitudes, recluse and woody banks, sweet-feeding springs, and all the charms that birds, grass, wild-flowers, rabbits and squirrels, and old walnut trees can bring." A favorite spot of observation was the Camden ferry-boat, upon which he would cross and recross the Delaware, absorbed in the spectacle of the day and night. At times he suffered pain, neglect, poverty; but, for the most part, the last years of his life were spent in the enjoyment of kindly associations and in fruitful labor. *Specimen Days* gives abundant evidence of an inward happiness, even though circumstances often combined against his serenity.

After surmounting three-score and ten,
With all their chances, changes, losses, sorrows,
My parents' death, the vagaries of my life, the many tearing passions of me, the war of '63 and '4,
As some old broken soldier, after a long, hot, wearying march, or haply after battle,
To-day at twilight, hobbling, answering company roll-call, *Here*, with vital voice,
Reporting yet, saluting yet, the Officer over all.

XII

It is a commonplace observation that *Leaves of Grass* abstracts a reader from parlors and libraries, but aims to bring him into the region of his own self-activity, in league with the great companions out of doors. The book contains a personality, and is freighted only to a very slight degree with the lore of libraries. Probably not a single learned or bookish allusion is to be found in the whole of *Leaves of Grass*. It would be a mistake, however, to conclude that Whitman was himself unacquainted with books. He imposed upon his readers by the assumption of his workmen's dress and his hostility to the conventional forms of culture, while pleading for the dignity of the simple man and the value of the culture of life. As a matter of fact, countless books went to the making of his point of view. His theory of inclusiveness contained the best things said and thought in the world. He who, of all men of the century, embodies most the modern movement of expansion, could not be partial in his preparation. He included the scholar no less than the workingman, and his subtle psychology and profound metaphysics and delicate mysticism afford abundant exercise to the scholastic mind. A poem like *Eidôlons* is unequivocal in asserting the supremacy of mind-images, "the entities of entities." Much as he pretended to contemn culture, he was himself its representative. Before 1855 he had read and pondered deeply the meaning of the Bible, Homer (which he knew almost by heart), Ossian, the ancient Hindu poems, Dante, the Greek dramatists, and Shakespeare. He had familiarized his spirit with theirs, and identified himself with their art. He affirms he sat studying long at the feet of the old masters, and this is literally true. Speaking of Shakespeare, he once said, "If I had not stood before these poems with uncovered head fully aware of their colossal grandeur and beauty of form and spirit, I could not have written *Leaves of Grass*." The great literatures served as a challenge. They taught him the one thing they can teach an original mind,—self-respect.

Dead poets, philosophs, priests,
Martyrs, artists, inventors, governments long since,
Language-shapers on other shores,
Nations once powerful, now reduced, withdrawn, or desolate,
I dare not proceed till I respectfully credit what you have left
    wafted hither,
I have perused it, own it is admirable, (moving awhile among it,)
Think nothing can ever be greater, nothing can ever deserve more
    than it deserves,
Regarding it all intently a long while, then dismissing it,
I stand in my place with my own day here.

At two periods of his life he was much absorbed in reading. In New York, during the years preceding the first edition of his poems, he was an omnivorous reader, and brought himself fully in touch with the drift of thought at the time. He read newspapers . and magazines to keep closer to the people. He read in libraries; and, on the event of an outing to the woods or sea, he would carry a book to provoke thought. The enormous scrap-books he made up at this time, containing articles on every subject, with passages underscored and commented upon, disclose the range and careful-

ness of his reading.   One of these books contains his own abstract
of the poem of the *Cid* and of the *Nibelungen Lied* and accounts
of Dante and the *Divine Comedy*.   A manuscript note indicates
the reading of the *Inferno* in 1859..   Among his memoranda ap-
pear directions to procure and read certain books,— as, " Get
Schiller's Complete Works."

Later at Camden, in the quiet of his seclusion, he again brought
himself abreast with the current thought.   Concerning his occu-
pation at Timber Creek in 1879, he wrote: " When I feel in the
mood I read and filter some book or piece or page or author
through my mind, amid these influences, in these surroundings.
Queer how new and different the books and authors appear in the
open air, with wind blowing and birds calling in the bushes and
you on the banks of the negligent pond.   I get some old edition of
no pecuniary value, and then take portions in my pocket.   In this
way I have dislocated the principal American writers of my time
— Emerson, Longfellow, Whittier, and the rest — with translations
of the French Madame Dudevant (always good to me), the Ger-
man metaphysician Hegel, and nearly all the current foreign
poets."

The fruits of much reading and meditation are discoverable in
his handling of scientific principles and philosophic formulas, in his
penetrative literary criticism, and in the sweeping generalizations
that illumine his prose writings.   Among his lifelong companions
were Scott's novels and *Border Minstrelsy*.   He had known the
Arabian Nights from boyhood.   He had read Emerson but casu-
ally before 1855, but later came to know him intimately.   George
Sand and Tennyson were prime favorites.   He was fond of recit-
ing *Ulysses*, and he looked the character.   A little poem of Mür-
ger's on Death had especial attractiveness.   Among the poems he
liked to recite were Schiller's *Diver*, *John Anderson*, Mürger's
Midnight Visitor, *The Bridge of Sighs*, *The Raven*, *The Passions*,
and *The Battle of Naseby*.   The sayings of Epictetus and Rous-
seau's *Confessions* were among his hand-books.   In his copy of
the Tragedies of Euripides is the memorandum: " Had this vol-
ume at Washington and thro' the war — also at Camden — alto-
gether all of 20 years."   From Poe he adopted the theory that
a poem should be short, the product of single emotions.   In one
important book he found many of his ideas corroborated.   This
was Felton's *Ancient and Modern Greece*, which he came upon at
the beginning of the war, and read innumerable times till he knew
it by heart.   Once in conversation with Sidney Morse he quoted

from Felton the following passage : " To the Greeks the natural man was not the savage running naked in the woods, but the man whose senses, imagination, and reason are unfolded in their highest reach ; whose bodily force and mental powers are in equipoise, and in full and beautiful action; who has the keenest eye, the surest hand, the truest ear, the richest voice, the loftiest and most rhythmical step; whose passions though strong are held in check, whose moral nature runs into no morbid perversions, and whose intellectual being is robustly developed ; whose life moves on in rhythmical accord with God, nature, and man, with no discord except to break its monotony and to be resolved in the harmony of its peaceful and painless close. This is the ideal being, whose nature is unfolded without disease, imperfection, or sin, to perpetual happiness and joy." No better description than this could be written of Whitman's ideal American. Many such passages might be gleaned from Whitman's scrap-books, which contain similar suggestive ideas. The chief fact, however, is the supremacy, amid all the books, of Whitman's self. That which he read was taken for verification to his own consciousness. As Horace Traubel says, " He was never cheated by books." His knowledge never appeared as pedantry, but was dissolved in the intelligence. If the reading of books made literature or if culture made genius, there would be no lack of these things in the world. Louis James Block describes in a poem to Whitman what seems to me to be the genuine sources of *Leaves of Grass* : —

God, who is Man at highest, and Nature that toils up to Man,
Dwelt in thy song and in thee,—
Not as involved in the garb of the dim and mouldering Past,
Not as in tomes and in tombs,
But truth, alive and afresh,
Flowing again in the mind
That gave up its life to be cleansed and refilled with its essences
  pure,
Bubbling anew in this late year of the world.

XIII

" Publish my name," said the poet, " and hang up my picture as that of the tenderest lover." Whitman had a passion for friends. Sympathy was his fundamental quality. The Calamus poems represent his " frailest leaves," yet his " strongest lasting." He had the rare faculty of drawing all men to him. " Over and above all ordinary greatness," said Dr. Bucke, in his funeral address, "Whitman had in an eminent degree that crowning endowment, faculty, quality, or whatever it may be called, the possession of which causes a man to be picked out from the rest and set apart as an object of affection. In his own vivid language, 'He has the pass-key of hearts, to him the response of the prying of hands on the knobs.'" Of this fact there are many testimonies. Dr. Bucke in 1877 first called upon the man whose poems he had read with delight and enthusiasm. Long after the interview he said of it: "It would be nothing more than the simple truth to state that I was by it lifted to and set upon a higher plane of existence, upon which I have more or less continuously lived ever since; that is, for a period of eighteen years. And my feeling toward the man, Walt Whitman, from that day to the present has been and is that of the deepest affection and reverence." The Rev. Moncure D. Conway visited Whitman on Long Island in 1865, and declared that after meeting him he went off to find himself almost sleepless with thinking of his new acquaintance. "He had so magnetized me," he said, "so charged me, as it were, with something indefinable, that for the time the only wise course of life seemed to be to put on a blue shirt and a blouse, and loaf about Mannahatta and Paumanok." And John Burroughs gives testimony: "To tell me that Whitman is not a large, fine, fresh, magnetic personality, making you love him and want always to be with him, were to tell me that my whole past life is a deception and all the impression of my perceptions a fraud." On Whitman's own part the love of men and women was a necessity of his nature. He compelled devotion. He yearned for sympathy. Emerson once asked him what he found in common people, and Thoreau put the same question: "What is there in the people? Pshaw! what do you (a man who sees as well as anybody) find in all this cheating political corruption?" The poet's answer is not recorded, but its substance may be found in his comment on Tennyson: "Tennyson seems to me to be a superb fellow; only with a personality such as his, what a pity not to give himself to men. A man cannot invest his capital better than in comradeship. Literary men and artists seem to shrink from companionship; to me it is exhilarating, affects me in the same way that the light or storm does." He fed upon the people as bees upon flowers. L. N. Fowler, the phrenologist, told him, "You are one of the friendliest men in the world, and your happiness is greatly dependent upon your social relations." Fortunately, his realized identities were well-nigh universal. Alma Johnston relates an incident of a visit Whitman made to some Indian prisoners in Kansas before the Civil War, in company with the governor of the State and some other officials. Some thirty Indians, all of them chiefs, were grouped in the jail yard, where they sullenly squatted, with their blankets wrapped around them. The governor and the officers were introduced to them, but not a savage moved. Then Whitman in his flannel shirt and his broad-brimmed hat stepped forward, and held out his hand. The leading chiefs looked at him for a moment, grasped his proferred hand with an emphatic "How!" and turned to the others. Thereupon the Indians rose and greeted him. "I suppose," explained Whitman, "they recognized the savage in me,—a comradeship to which their nature responded." It would be indeed impossible to exaggerate the affection yielded him by multitudes of persons of every class. Many of the friends of his life are nameless,— men in prisons, hospitals, and workshops, engineers, street-car drivers and conductors, the "help" on the ferries and pilot boats, omnibus drivers, and, above all, the soldiers of the war. The affection existing between him and these men can hardly be understood, much less described. Only one instance of his "manly attachment" is given permanent record in the letters to Peter Doyle, his "dear son," "dear boy Pete." These were men he attracted simply by his personality, who did not know he had ever written a line of poetry or who, if they knew, like Pete Doyle, "did not know what he was trying to get at." He entered into their employments with a cheery, "Come, boys, tell me all about it," and by his yearning for experience and affection drew the thought out of their minds and the love out of their hearts. For all he would do many services. One winter in New York he drove an omnibus, taking the place of a sick driver in the hospital. It was his custom in Washington to present the street-car drivers with warm gloves for their winter work. He was friendly with all whom he met. Here in a poem is "a glimpse through an interstice caught"

Of a crowd of workmen and drivers in a bar-room around the stove late of a winter night, and I unremark'd seated in a corner,

Of a youth who loves me and whom I love, silently approaching and seating himself near, that he may hold me by the hand,

A long while amid the noises of coming and going, of drinking and oath and smutty jest,

There we two, content, happy in being together, speaking little, perhaps not a word.

In the New York days all the literary men knew and liked him. A deeply felt attachment grew up with Emerson, Thoreau, and Alcott. Stedman, John Swinton, and Charles Eldridge were close friends. Bryant would accompany him on long walks. At Washington he was a familiar figure. Lincoln was at once impressed by his presence, and thought that here, at length, was a genuine man. Garfield always welcomed him with a salute and the quotation, "After all not to create only." He formed lifelong friendships with William D. O'Connor and John Burroughs, who became his stanchest defenders. Long, lonely days followed upon his paralysis in 1873, when at Camden, sick and in isolation, unrecognized and almost neglected, he suffered three dark years. After several months of residence in Camden, he wrote pathetically to Doyle: "I don't know a soul here,— am entirely alone — sometimes sit alone and think, for two hours on a stretch — have not formed a single acquaintance here, any ways intimate." He records the visit of Mr. Ingram from Philadelphia: "He came over and hunted for hours through the hot sun, found me at last — he evidently thought I was keeled up and hard up, and he came to offer help — he has been a great traveller, is English by birth — I found him good company, and was glad to see him — he has been twice — so you see there are good souls left." But in 1876 recognition came from England. "Those blessed gales from the British Island probably (certainly) saved me," the poet confessed. A letter had been sent to the English press, written by Robert Buchanan, stating the poet's needs; and a hearty response followed from hundreds of English authors who promptly purchased his books and sent emotional cheer. To John Addington Symonds, from his youth up, Whitman had been the medium of a regenerated life; and Symonds' letters to his "master" offer the tribute of a disciple's affection. An acquaintance with Tennyson began in 1870, and a correspondence was kept up between them till Whitman's death. One of the last letters written by Tennyson was a note of thanks to a correspondent in America who had sent him notice of Whitman's death. Concerning this relationship Whitman wrote in 1876, "I am not at all sure that Alfred Tennyson *sees my poems;* . . . but I think *he sees me,* and nothing could have evidenced more courtesy and manliness and hospitality than his letters to me have shown for five years." Edward Carpenter came over in 1877 for the express purpose of meeting his great friend. A most beautiful and intimate comradeship sprang up with Anne Gilchrist, who had written in 1870 "A Woman's Estimate of Walt Whitman," the most courageous and appreciative essay that had been written of Whitman up to that time. During a visit to America in 1876 she came to know Whitman personally, and he fully realized the ideal she had formed from the poems. She wrote to a friend, "He brings such an atmosphere of cordiality and geniality with him as is indescribable"; and warmer tributes follow. Whitman said on his part, "Among the perfect women I have known (and it has been my remarkably good fortune to have had the very best for mother, sister, and friends), I have known none more perfect in every relation than my dear, dear friend, Anne Gilchrist." And at her death he wrote, "Nothing now remains but a sweet and rich memory,— none more beautiful all time, all life, all the earth." After 1876 the Calamus battle was pretty well gained. No man ever had more or warmer friends. Bucke, Harned, Traubel, Mr. and Mrs. Johnston, Kennedy, Ingersoll, O'Reilly, Donaldson, and many others were his lovers and comrades. Joaquin Miller, Joel Chandler Harris, Bret Harte, Mark Twain, Hamlin Garland, and all the Western men came to recognize the Camden Sage as their fellow and leader. The press became more lenient. *The Critic*, under the direction of Richard Watson Gilder, gave the poet fair treatment and honor. From all parts of Europe came tokens of love. At the time of Whitman's death, in 1892, his yearning for comrades was fully gratified. He was one of the Great Companions.

From these relationships this poet, beyond a doubt, derived his greatest strength and wisdom. As he himself was a new type of man,— a man who was wholly love, who could not harbor hate or jealousy,— so his book is a new type of book,— a book that not only has love as its ground and plan, but that also requires the comprehension of love from the reader.

Thou reader throbbest life and pride and love the same as I,
Therefore for thee the following chants.